THE KRAKEN VS. THE LOCH NESS MONSTER

by Alberto Rayo

CAPSTONE PRESS
a capstone imprint

Published by Capstone Press, an imprint of Capstone
1710 Roe Crest Drive, North Mankato, Minnesota 56003
capstonepub.com

Copyright © 2026 by Capstone. All rights reserved. No part of this publication may be reproduced in whole or in part, or stored in a retrieval system, or transmitted in any form or by any means, electronic, mechanical, photocopying, recording, or otherwise, without written permission of the publisher.

Library of Congress Cataloging-in-Publication Data is available on the Library of Congress website.

ISBN: 9798875225765 (hardcover)
ISBN: 9798875225710 (paperback)
ISBN: 9798875225727 (ebook PDF)

Summary: Two huge sea creatures face off in a fierce fight. The Kraken and the Loch Ness Monster are very similar cryptids, but only one will come out on top.

Editorial Credits
Editor: Ashley Kuehl; Designer: Hilary Wacholz; Media Researcher: Rebekah Hubstenberger; Production Specialist: Tori Abraham

Image Credits
Alamy: VICTOR HABBICK VISIONS/SCIENCE PHOTO LIBRARY, cover (bottom), 19; Capstone: Jon Hughes, 27 (loch ness monster head); Getty Images: iStock/4ek, 25, iStock/sabelskaya, 17, iStock/the8monkey, 14 (tentacles), iStock/Елена Бабенкова, 12, J Studios, 14 (whale), John M Lund Photography Inc, 13, Kurt Miller/Stocktrek Images, 15, VICTOR HABBICK VISIONS, 23, VICTOR HABBICK VISIONS/SCIENCE PHOTO LIBRARY, 9; Science Source: Victor Habbick Visions, 20-21; Shutterstock: Amir Dayyan, 27 (background), cammep, 29 (crown), Daniel Eskridge, 24, Dirk-Jan de Graaf, 6, Fer Gregory, 5 (bottom), Kalleeck, 5 (top), Kitoumi, cover (top), 29 (kraken), LOMAKIN, 7, 27 (tentacles), Superstock: Jerry Lofaro/Stocktrek Images/StockTrek, 10-11

Design Elements
Shutterstock: Ballerion, Foxy Fox, Nadiinko

Any additional websites and resources referenced in this book are not maintained, authorized, or sponsored by Capstone. All product and company names are trademarks™ or registered® trademarks of their respective holders

TABLE OF CONTENTS

UNDERWATER CLASH! 4

SEA MONSTERS UP CLOSE. 8

CLOSE COUSINS 16

SWIMMING WITH PLESIOSAURS 18

SECOND ROUND, START! 22

GOTCHA! 26

Glossary 30
Read More 31
Internet Sites 31
Index 32
About the Author 32

Words in **bold** are in the glossary.

UNDERWATER CLASH!

Waves crash on the North Sea. Late at night, a huge **tentacle** pokes up from the cold, dark water. It tosses a creature into the air. The creature lets out a screech.

It's the Loch Ness Monster. Her body falls back into the sea, and she escapes. The tentacle belongs to the Kraken. His prey has escaped, but this fight will continue!

Name: Loch Ness Monster

Alias: Nessie

Type of Cryptid: Eel, sea snake, or **extinct** water reptile

First Sighting: 565 CE

Range (Area): Loch Ness, Scotland

Likes: Fish, privacy

Dislikes: Crowded places

Name: Kraken

Aliases: Scylla

Type of Cryptid: Giant squid

First Sighting: 1180 CE

Range (Area): Norwegian Sea, between Norway and Ireland

Likes: Causing mischief to sailors

Dislikes: Boats, sperm whales

SEA MONSTERS UP CLOSE

Nessie is the most famous resident of Scotland's Loch Ness. This lake happens to connect to the sea. So she can come and go.

The first story about this **cryptid** dates all the way back to Ireland in 565 CE! We know she has a long neck. Those who have seen her say she's long and thin. Some say she looks like an eel. Others describe her as a sea snake.

FACT

Arthur Grant saw Nessie jump into a lake in 1934. His drawing of her became famous.

THE KRAKEN AWAKENS

Think of a big squid. Now think way bigger. The Kraken is a huge **cephalopod**. He's probably between 40 to 60 feet (12.2 to 18.3 meters) long. But he might be up to 100 feet (30.5 m) long!

The Kraken lives alone, deep in the Norwegian Sea. In stories from the 1200s, he often attacked Viking ships.

FACT
A Norwegian book from 1755 says the Kraken's body would be 1.5 miles (2.4 kilometers) around!

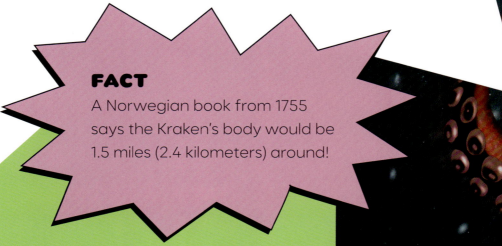

BEST BEHAVIOR

Nessie is shy and elusive. She rarely attacks humans.

The Kraken is mostly known as a villain for heroes to defeat. Maybe that's because of his size and the many stories of him destroying ships.

DEEP-SEA DIET

Nessie probably eats fish. That makes her a **pescatarian**.

The Kraken eats fish too. But he's so big that he needs to eat much more. He may hunt large ocean creatures, such as sharks, squids, and even whales!

FACT
Nessie may swim to the open ocean to hunt. She can find more food there.

CLOSE COUSINS

Many people believe the Kraken might be related to the giant squid. This creature was discovered back in 1856. That means the Kraken could have the same features. Those include a sharp beak, two large eyes, two tentacles, eight arms, and an ink sac!

FACT
It's not the Kraken, but the giant squid can grow to about 40 feet (12 m) long!

SWIMMING WITH PLESIOSAURS

Some people believe Nessie is a **plesiosaur**. This aquatic creature went extinct millions of years ago . . . or did it? If this theory is true, Nessie is a really old reptile. She may have survived because Loch Ness is so **isolated**.

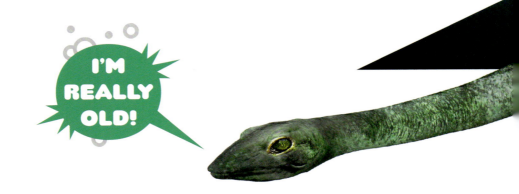

I'M REALLY OLD!

Nessie is 20 to 30 feet (6.1 to 9.1 m) long. That's as tall as a three-story house. She has a long, muscular neck. Her four large flippers help her swim fast. She doesn't have claws or horns. But she does have a strong, dangerous bite!

SECOND ROUND, START!

Nessie has learned from the first fight. She comes during the day. She stays near the surface to **bait** her opponent. The Kraken is ready to attack. But he must wait until Nessie gets closer. The first part of the battle is about patience.

HIDDEN TRICKS

The Kraken takes the bait. The huge squid swims toward Nessie and the surface. As he reaches her, the sun blinds him. Nessie readies her attack: a fierce bite on the Kraken's body.

But he's got a secret weapon. It's called ink attack! The ink turns the water into a black soup.

GOTCHA!

The Kraken's eyes are used to the inky water. But Nessie cannot see. The Kraken catches her with two large tentacles. This fight should be over, but Nessie refuses to pass out.

Nessie's body is stronger than the Kraken's tentacles. Her long neck lets her bite the Kraken's body again. One of them must give in!

A VICTORY . . . THIS TIME

The Kraken releases her and prepares a follow-up attack. But Nessie is gone. She can't beat the Kraken in this battle, but she can run. The Kraken will wait for her return. Both know the Kraken wins this round.

IT'S OVER! THE KRAKEN WINS!

WAS THIS FIGHT FAIR? Could Nessie win with the right strategy? What do you think happens when

the Kraken and the Loch Ness Monster CLASH?

GLOSSARY

bait (BAYT)—to attract an animal or to put out something that attracts an animal

cephalopod (SEF-uh-luh-pod)—an ocean animal that has tentacles attached to its head

cryptid (KRIP-tihd)—a creature whose existence has not been proven

extinct (ik-STINGKT)—having died out

isolated (EYE-suh-lay-tid)—far away from other people or things

pescatarian (pes-kuh-TAIR-ee-uhn)—an animal that eats fish but not other kinds of meat

plesiosaur (PLEE-see-uh-sawr)—a large meat-eating reptile from the Mesozoic era

tentacle (TEN-tuh-kuhl)—a long limb on some animals, such as squid or octopus

READ MORE

Harper, Benjamin. *The Secret Life of the Loch Ness Monster.* North Mankato, MN: Capstone Press, 2023.

Hubbard, Ben. *What Do We Know About the Kraken?* New York: Penguin Workshop, 2024.

Trinick, Loveday. *Oceanarium: Welcome to the Museum.* Somerville, MA: Candlewick Press, 2022.

INTERNET SITES

American Museum of Natural History: Marine Biology
amnh.org/explore/ology/marine-biology

Britannica Kids: Loch Ness Monster
kids.britannica.com/students/article/Loch-Ness-monster/631551

National Geographic Kids: Giant Squid
kids.nationalgeographic.com/animals/invertebrates/facts/giant-squid

INDEX

giant squid, 7, 16, 24
Grant, Arthur, 9

Kraken
  first sighting, 7
  food, 14
  ink, 16, 25
  nicknames, 7
  range, 7, 10
  size, 10, 13
  tentacles, 4, 16, 26
  type of cryptid, 7, 10, 16

Loch Ness Monster
  age, 18
  first sighting, 6, 8

food, 6, 14, 15
long neck, 8, 20, 26
nicknames, 6
range, 6, 8, 15
size, 8, 20
type of cryptid, 6, 8, 18

Norwegian Sea, 7, 10

plesiosaur, 18

Scotland, 6, 8
ships, 10, 13

Vikings, 10

ABOUT THE AUTHOR

Alberto Rayo is a writer from Lima, Perú. He loves science fiction that feels like fantasy, fantasy that feels like science fiction, and monsters (because they're cooler than humans). When he's not writing comics, he's writing prose. And when he's not writing prose, he might be sleeping.